MISSIVES
FROM THE
UNIVERSE

MISSIVES
FROM THE
UNIVERSE

A Companion to Awakening

Dolly Hall

Ethereal Expressions
PUBLISHING

www.etherealexpressions.com

First printing 2014
ISBN 978-0-615-90571-6
LCCN 2013951978

Dedication

To Bill, my husband, best friend
and guardian spirit

To our sons, Alex, Mark and Kevin,
our favorite teachers

And to souls everywhere growing home.

Acknowledgements

To my parents, Lonnie and Ruth Guess,
whose love of learning inspired me
to awaken

Awakening

The process of awakening repeatedly attracts souls to the physical plane, resuming the journey before time. Circumstances, trials and triumphs return as energy accumulated through eons of living. Again and again the soul returns to the physical plane to experience the oneness of the Universe as a reality. Trial and error gradually initiate the awakening process.

The moment dawns when the soul perceives itself capable of significant expansion. Relinquishing conformity, it struggles to experience the reality of a burgeoning wisdom. Ultimately a path of no return, commitment to this longing forever alters the landscape of its being.

Tentatively accepting the Universe as its source and teacher, the soul is tutored in unconditional acceptance of inner guidance. As the divine whisper is repeatedly embraced, soul/mind begins to intuit deeper messages in the rhythm of daily life. Appearances begin to speak their hidden meanings.

Inspired from within, the soul surrenders the burden of ego attachment and re-orients to the meaning of its journey. Coupled with the intelligence of the Universe, the earthly sojourn assumes new dimensions, revealing a shimmer of light in a sea of darkness. A guide appears to lead you. Follow.

> Choice is the path.
> Understanding is the slope.
> Awakening is the journey and
> Ascension the destination.

Nature's Way

Trusting growth to the wisdom of the Universe, the caterpillar neither doubts nor fears what it hears. It believes. Intuitively following inner urges, the caterpillar attunes to ideas of life beyond lowly existence.

Forgoing attachment to the past, it enters the daring process of transformation and willingly penetrates a landscape of darkness. Accompanied only by commitment, it cautiously adapts to a labyrinth both strange and unfamiliar. Inner silence guides the process and encourages the inner vision. This unwavering concentration eventually severs the past completely. Memories lose their attachment and the caterpillar accepts oneness with the greater life that created it. Turmoil increases, then ceases. Asleep to the world, powerful transforming energies consume the shell of what used to be and delicately forge a new path.

Prolonged quiescence eventually stirs, inducing gradual awakening. New consciousness emerges, vibrant wings unfold, and pedestrian limitations are forgotten.

A whisper gently nudges the new creature to embrace its budding destiny. "I am your wings. Trust me—fly." Believing the whisper, it flies.

Such is the journey of awakening.

Nothing is personal and nothing is out of place.

This is Nature's message to man.

~ The Universe

U•ni•verse

1. The oneness of all existence
2. The divine intelligence that manifests consciousness
3. The infinity of Life
4   The eternal moment
5. The flow of Evolution

Every life is determined by its relationship to this dynamic energy. Referred to here as the Universe, this ubiquitous power informs and unfolds each according to their instructions.

Beliefs you hold to be true are your instructions.

The day arrives when recurring circumstances finally bring you face-to-face with the age-old question, "What would life be like if I truly understood it?"

Wisdom responds, "Life will always be precisely what it is, but you can know peace in spite of what it is—and this, in the measure that you desire it."

The gift of will is man's only true possession; it is the faculty that determines all experiences. A creative vehicle, it allows man to accept or separate from divine consciousness, choosing the reality he wishes to have.

The Universe connects with man through the medium of this will, assuring experiences that reflect the will that is chosen. A man's world mirrors his habits of attention.

Free will is the greatest show on earth.

Its freedom consists of allowing every man to create the reality he chooses to believe, and this experience happens everywhere at the same time.

Hence, the greatest show on earth.

The primary lesson of Life is learning to trust the eternal principle that balances the visible with the invisible.

Captivated by the world, the personality remains oblivious to the messages behind the world. Unknowingly, worldly judgment designs each lesson to be learned—too often the same one.

In the end, life challenges are found to be stumbling blocks created by the personality for the experience of overcoming them and remembering its true self.

Each has the right to embrace what he accepts as true. In fact, he cannot do otherwise, for the mind only embraces what it understands, thereafter experiencing it.

Judging another's path is futile, for Universal Law mandates strict balance between a person's focus and his experiences. Regardless of the issue at hand, the Universe addresses it spontaneously—and perfectly.

Much emphasis is placed on the importance of living in the moment. Less is placed on the how and the why.

Universal wisdom unfolds itself moment-to-moment. Forever surrounding you, it happens as the reality of the moment.

Refusing to censor the Universe is the only way to attain the peace that passes all understanding. This choice aligns you with the flow of natural fulfillment, which only reveals itself in the moment.

Divine Law is the embryo of soul growth. The growth rate, however, is the soul's own choice.

Souls return to the physical plane to resume their journey of expansion, otherwise known as growth. Delay results from failure to understand that "problems" are necessary opportunities to reverse the thinking that caused the problem. The soul's response to these opportunities accelerates or impedes the growth process.

Each day is an opportunity to discover your center and live from it.

When you cease to demand that events conform to personal wishes and learn to trust divine wisdom, you enter the reality of your Universal self. This state of mind is your center and the reason you have returned to the earth plane.

Hidden from awareness is an entity called 'the i.'

With stealth, it adopts your identity as its own and asserts judgments into every event unfolding in your life. Always threatened, it conveys an uneasy feeling that something is wrong, followed by, "i or they need to remedy this situation."

It promises certain fulfillment if you follow its demands, but the promise is empty. Its sole agenda is to prevent peace of mind by churning the mind from one distraction to another, opposing natural serenity and contentment. Undetected and unopposed, the i is confident of its safety—for who examines the contents of their own mind?

The original identity thief, the i moves best when the mind is asleep to its activity. Awakening is the remedy.

Use every free moment
to strengthen your connection to the Universe.

And every moment is free.

Folly attaches to experiences
while intellect manipulates experiences
but only wisdom understands them.

Mind expands or contracts according to ideas
culled from experiences. Each is a teacher, a
uniquely designed learning tool—nothing more,
nothing less.

Nothing in the Universe is personal. A supremely intelligent energy, Life pervades all space without exception, bias or censure, manifesting in form what exists in the soul.

Physical reality is the offspring of spiritual reality. As such, life is fair, but fair is misunderstood.

Your relationship to the Universe is a summary of responses to your experiences. Though responses appear to be many, there are actually only two, understanding or misunderstanding.

Stubbornly refusing to learn is the single act that separates a soul from the purpose of its lessons. Learning acceptance is the way out. In a state of acceptance, the mind accepts responsibility for creating its experiences. Such insight represents growth and negates the need for another occurrence. Misunderstanding assures the experience will return again and again. Responses are recorded in the soul's DNA.

Communication

takes place when unspoken words are heard, silent intentions understood, and a course of action evident.

Discerning energy is the basis of true communication. Where lengthy discourse is necessary, communication is replaced with mere words.

From this day forward, release others

from your expectations of who they should be or how they should live. An amazing thing will happen—emotional burdens suddenly drop away.

Freed from responsibility that was never yours, clarity shows that Universal balance places everything where it needs to happen when it needs to happen—for soul evolution.

Learning from your own intuitive promptings assures creative and timely progress.

Ignoring your own path binds you to the prison of imitation, guaranteeing failure to grow beyond the limitation of others.

Feelings accurately mirror your inner state of mind. They reveal your belief system. Contrary to popular belief, feelings are not caused by circumstances but are the cause of them.

You only feel what you believe, and the Universe responds to you by obeying your beliefs. This invisible shift attracts and repels the people, places and things that form the fabric of your life. Your feelings are more important than you know.

Relationships are

opportunities that reveal your feelings about yourself. As an example, when you refuse to accept yourself, notice how often you plead, expect or even demand acceptance from others. But it doesn't happen—for an internal problem is never fixed with an external solution.

Failing to honor yourself strongly attracts relationships that also fail to honor you. For a while each will camouflage your lack of confidence, but in time must betray your misplaced trust. Unerringly, the Universe delivers your energy back to you. Accepting your own validity creates relationships that mirror this acceptance.

There is no error in spontaneous impersonal action. Error does not enter until you personalize the action.

You are a particle of omniscient, omnipotent Life shaping itself to the needs of each moment. This truth frees you from obligatory interactions, for there is never a moment that Life does not know where it's going or what it's doing.

Renounce frustration when learning the way of wisdom, for learning is an acquired taste.

Trained by what it pays attention to, mind must leave its comfort zone to expand itself. But the mind must be trained to leave its comfort zone. New habits must be practiced beyond the level of discomfort. Commitment is the habit that causes an ideal to manifest.

There is nothing personal in the Universe. Each day you create tomorrow while receiving yesterday.

It's all impersonal Law responding to your beliefs.

Pray daily:

"Lord of my being, thank you for your plans this day, which need to happen for my growth and are best for my growth."

Your responses during the day give you an indication of your growth.

Professing love begs the question, "How do you know it is love?"

Love is the riddle of Life, owned by none yet giving to all. It directs itself impersonally and unconditionally, remaining free of the need to prove itself. You love because you know how to love.

Personalities *love* for a host of other personal reasons.

Worrying over calamities that "might" happen results from mistrusting Universal order and balance. Worry believes that peace of mind depends on a desired outcome. But peace of mind depends on aligning with the harmony of the Universe, which is the art of impersonal thinking. Holding to personal opinions is a guarantee that peace of mind will remain beyond your grasp.

Take control of your life. Let go your attachments. Nothing in life belongs to you but your thoughts. Life belongs to the harmony of itself, which it achieves perfectly moment-to-moment. Worry less about what Life is doing and focus more on what you are doing. If misaligned with the flow of Life, you assure calamity by attracting the balance of inharmonious thoughts.

*A*ttention addicted to future outcomes fails to acknowledge the secret of success, which is attention to the present.

Now is the only reality. From moment-to-moment, this-now-to-the-next-now, the time is always the present. What you desire must be felt as a reality "now." Train yourself to feel the achievement of your efforts. The feeling must be "present" before the Universe grants the desire. The Universe helps those who help themselves.

Love is all there is.

The Universe manifests love by unconditional
acceptance of every inner reality.
This unconditional acceptance neither favors nor
forsakes, but manifests all exactly as chosen.
In this way, Love appears everywhere at once.

If bored or trapped in a sea of inertia, there is
a guaranteed escape. Create. Creation opens the
trap door.

An imprisoned Spirit stifles the body with
lethargy, but constructive activity immediately
sets it free. A consummate artist, Spirit loves to
create on the canvas it created. You.

T*he* soul endlessly defines its boundaries by experimenting with beliefs about itself.

When beliefs manifest, they are experienced as feelings.

Feelings are the result of what the mind is thinking. Pay attention to them. They are text messages from the soul, communicating whether it's expanding or contracting.

T*here* is no error in impersonal action. But misunderstanding enters when an action is separated from its cause.

It is impersonal action that achieves Universal balance. Uncensored, such action creates "upward" balance or "downward" balance depending on the instructions it is given. Either way, it is answering a request. This is the cause behind what you see.

You are a level of awareness defined only by thoughts you choose to accept. Thoughts repeatedly selected consolidate into beliefs, which manifest as your outer life.

Each day is a journey through opportunities of your own making. Doors open or remain stuck depending on whether you believe you can walk through. Study your habitual thinking. There are the keys to each door.

When truth unfolds from within—mind is born into a higher realm of understanding. These are natural birth-days and cause for celebration.

When the mind is lifted, it soars to an unspeakable moment of ecstasy, experienced in the heart as joy. Traditional birthdays are symbolic of this jubilant flight.

Only the reasonable learn by reason.
Pain is the other instructor.
But when you choose the discipline of pain
You earn what you learn at the foot of a master
And great indeed is the wisdom thereafter.

Disagreeing with what happens in the moment causes suffering only to the degree that you disagree. Then you will learn. That is the only purpose of the pain.

Life is pro-choice.

Free will guarantees it.

Each must learn the way each must learn
And each must choose his own way.

Every soul manifests what it needs to learn the way it needs to learn it.

Guilt is a very beneficial emotion but only at your expense.

Self-negation fails to recognize and accept your innate power and gives others permission to take advantage of your confusion. Guilt is a sure sign of low self-esteem and is almost always manipulated by others.

Learning to love yourself is the lesson that guilt teaches. Loving yourself frees you from the chains that bind.

Never alone, you are always surrounded by thoughts you habitually entertain, returning to you clothed as personalities harboring similar thought patterns. This is your natural family, and every day is a reunion.

The Universe is family-oriented, keeping you in close association with those whose beliefs closely match your own. Be not misled—when you choose your beliefs, you choose your family.

Stability is not found in a world where appearances ebb and flow with every tide. What promises to remain never does.

Eternal rhythms resist both time and change. Anchoring to this permanence is the path to stability.

The more you run from a problem
The more you multiply the problem.

Every flight invites new breeding ground, for the problem resides within you. Unless understood, there is no place that it will not appear.

It is not selfish to want to live your own life. Selfish is attempting to live someone else's.

Your life is a series of messages addressed to you and you alone. The same is true for your neighbor. Interfering with messages addressed to another is an act of supreme arrogance. You are not wiser than the law of cause and effect. Your selfishness prevents another from receiving messages that hold answers to their life.

No one needs you more than you do.

Your growth is all that you share with another. No matter what their need, your response will not exceed your wisdom. Helping yourself is the way to help others.

Life lessons are uniquely tailored to the mind creating the need for them. Thus, every path is individualized and though it may influence another, it can never be forced to do so.

The Universe demands that each design his own.

You cannot go past
What you must grow past.
Shortcuts are an illusion.

Mind is unlimited, but doubting this natural
magnificence reduces a powerful giant to the
stature of an ineffectual elf. The elf's name is
"**i**." To compensate and bolster confidence, the
i stages responses that never amount to more
than a hindrance of the mind's expansion. It is
the **i** that you must grow past.

*T*o err is human;
Understanding error is divine.

Error believes itself separate from the Laws of
the Universe and seeks to establish its own.
Since this cannot be done, it will not be. The
divine plan uses human error to teach universal
understanding.

Cause and effect meet in every
experience.

No moment arrives unbidden. Each moment
arrives or departs according to accumulated
choices. Yours.

Every moment is born of wisdom higher than your own.

Do not question the moment.
Question your understanding of it.

No person truly despises another;
It is their growth pattern despised.

And yet, like yourself, they are growing exactly the way they need to—to reach the same destination. Your judgment does not affect their growth but delays your own arrival time.

No matter what moment arrives, Love prepared its appearance. The Universe loves what you love.

Your moments unfold solely for you to experience what your beliefs feel like. Unknowingly, you create your moments.

Love is the only power in the Universe, though known by many names.

An active principle, Love assures that every mind receives what it loves. (Mind loves habitual thinking)

The Law is my shepherd.
I shall not plead.
For the Law only listens
To the voice of my deeds
And delivers unerringly
The choices I believe.

Faith is what you do, regardless of what
you say. It is the voice that communicates with
the Law of your being. It informs the Law of your
favorite thinking.

What you want and
what you say you want
are rarely the same thing.
One you believe and
the other you would like to believe;
your actions will show the difference.

Action always follows belief.

Events in your life result from what
you tell yourself when you are not listening. Your
feelings are messengers alerting you to inner
dialogues taking place at a deep level.

For heaven's sake, eavesdrop!

You can only know what you experience,
making all experience an opportunity
for greater knowing.

Thus, all paths are valid.

The entity you know as yourself is an
accumulation of the life thread that is you.
Meandering through lifetimes, your thread flows
as a seamless garment of evolution, becoming
knotted only when you forget how to flow.

When consciousness is distressed, it is because
it encounters a knot blocking the experience
of harmony. Progress is halted until the knot is
untangled. Knots surface whenever you think
the Universe should be doing other than what
it is doing. Remember who is wiser—and flow
impersonally.

It is not meant that another should save you but that you should learn to save yourself.

None can save you from your own free will, which empowers or imprisons. You create experiences that teach you how to best use your free will. If someone else saves you, be aware that you have not been saved.

Trust the balance of Universal Law and Be not dismayed by passing events. Every moment is balanced with wisdom.

Who among you is wiser?

Your life is a book;
Everything is part of the story.
The plot is about understanding
Who you are
And why you are
Where you are.

Beliefs write volumes about adventures in
free will.

You won't go before your time
And you won't stay after it.
No matter how wrong you think it may be,
The roster of death is not man's to see.
Transition is the aim when death makes a claim.
Evolution is the power that names the hour.

At the time of transition, the life thread adopts
its original non-material existence. After that, the
journey continues.

Consciousness

withdraws focus from the physical form when it is ready to undergo its next change of existence. All Nature is a template for this change.

Life forever shifts between visible and invisible existence. When the eye cannot see Life, it is called death. Yet death is the only change Life cannot know. The Life of nature perennially comes, goes, then returns as predictable seasons. Mankind, as a part of the same Life, likewise follows the same cycles.

What does not happen
Was not sufficiently believed.
What does—was.

Belief is a powerful magnet that attracts to itself what it believes, simultaneously repelling what it does not. Therefore, whatever you see is exactly what must be.

You are forever meeting unfinished business so you can finish it.

Failing to do so creates the drama of making others responsible for your liabilities. Since others are not responsible, they cannot and will not resolve your issues. Insisting that they do initiates and prolongs heartbreaking drama.

The key to manifestation lies in
Holding fast to faith
Until the mind believes
What faith is holding.

You'll see it when you believe it.

Detachment from the Universe is the origin of stress.

To understand this process, monitor the number of times you disagree with Life's unfolding moments, insisting that events be otherwise. Notice the dis-ease that fills you. Now multiply this by the years of your life, now and before. This is the number of times you have separated from oneness with the Universe.

Stress is the symptom of this separation and accumulates into every ill imaginable.

The sea of consciousness is interrelated, each part affecting another. By the Law of Attraction, energy automatically gravitates to others with corresponding mental energy.

When the mind is imprisoned, it imprisons others.
Freeing the mind frees others.

The quality of life's wholeness depends on your contribution.

Change in your outer world results spontaneously from change in your inner world.

Your inner world is your consciousness, a unique vibration that determines all the details of your life.

As the author of your inner world, you alone have the power to change it. And this, according to your relationship with the Universe. You either accept its wisdom or reject it. This free-will choice accumulates as your vibration, signaling circumstances that either accept your aspirations or reject them.

There is no other way.

The trick to having anything is giving it to yourself, for what you would possess must first be possessed in the mind.

"To him that hath, more will be given. To him that hath not, even that which he hath shall be taken away . . ."

The moment of exit from the physical plane is determined by a soul's accumulated choices.

So is the moment of entry.

The Law is a loyal servant that gives and
never takes.
It awaits the command of your beliefs and
guarantees
" . . . Thy will be done on earth as it is in
heaven . . ."

And it always is.

Birth and death are twin movements of
one Spirit.
At birth, Spirit creates form
To experience the outer world
While remembering the inner world.
At transition, form returns to Spirit
To review how well it remembered.

Mastering the memory is the purpose of the
journey.

When you truly love another
You accept the wisdom of their soul's evolution,

Not your idea of what their evolution should be.

Angst over another's life pattern is
a sure sign of misunderstanding the growth
process.
And it is neither wise nor helpful to challenge
the wisdom of growth. You will not win.

By accepting growth patterns, you channel the
very light sought by those suffering. This light
knows where to go. Rest in the knowledge that a
healing is taking place—starting with you.

You are always having in your life
What you are having in your mind.
This activity is either constructive or destructive,
Working for you—or against you.

Others are not to blame.

The Universe always catches you,
But only after you jump.

The leap is an affirmation of faith.

Leaping is symbolic of total surrender to the guidance of the Divine with full assurance of protection.

You will be caught.

Far from haphazard, Life is a perfectly ordered system of unfolding Law. Unfortunately, consciousness is often haphazard.

Therefore, by Law, the only thing that can happen is what you see happening.

Confusion seeks answers where they cannot be found.

But from whence arises the stronghold of confusion?

Nowhere but judgments and opinions about the wisdom of unfolding moments.

Judgments and opinions arise from erroneous beliefs.

Remove these veils and answers appear.

Learning never comes too late. It can only happen when it is time.

When you're ready, it is time.

The paradox of growth is that you must go backward in order to go forward, backing yourself out of what you walked into. Your ability to do this is the measure of your growth.

Understanding the role of limiting thoughts is most of the solution. Practicing surrender achieves it.

When a goal is chosen, mental actions
follow the choice.
When mental actions are absent, that is the goal.

Accepting or rejecting intentions toward a
goal releases energy that attracts or repels
the aspiration. The body obeys the thoughts
accepted, because power resides in acceptance.

Healing is the most profound of all aspirations. Though concentrated vigilance marks this training, all must accomplish a single requisite. Heal thyself.

But do not confuse healing with the practice of medicine.

Healing your separation from Source is the reason you're here, the mastery of which elevates the soul and restores health to the mind and body.

The practice of medicine is a worldly art for recalibrating the body—with scant regard for the deeper symptoms of the soul.

If healing does not take place in the soul, healing does not take place.

Decline the opportunity to blindly commit to another's path. Imitation of others will never satisfy your journey and, in all probability, significantly lengthen it.

Growth demands attention to your own unique lessons.

Change is predicated on thoughts you are prepared to change rather than activity you are prepared to change.

Changing activity merely duplicates the activity under a new name.

Mental activity automatically governs outer activity. If nothing above changes, nothing below changes.

When in doubt,
Follow Life's natural example:
Love without attaching,
Experience without judging and
Trust without doubt.

The Universe is all that ever comes to you—
albeit wearing many faces. Animate or
inanimate, all emerges from this source. Notice
when you stray from Life's natural example.
One of the faces has tricked you into accepting
suffering.

You never recover from an imagined injustice until you learn its lesson.

Cause-and-effect is all that happens in the world. Forever balanced, this principle assures justice in all interactions. Imagining injustice is just that. Learning that you are imagining is the lesson.

To achieve a desire, constantly expect it. If neither time, circumstance nor challenge dilutes your expectation, the desire will arrive.

Contrary to the general consensus, achievement happens inwardly before appearing outwardly.

Maintaining faith is the ultimate achievement.

Life is all about you and the relationships you create. People, places and things are your own united kingdom.

Each is under your rule and presents only when summoned.

It really is all about you.

To truly hear others,
Listen to their actions:
Actions carry a greater energy than words.

What you do is what you say.

All are born with the talent for allowing Spirit to express in the world. No matter the venue, when allowed, Spirit never fails to confer natural competence and confidence to its benefactor. These blessings encourage one to pay attention to their calling.

Do not discount your abilities. Spirit is showing your natural path to fulfillment as well as a blessing others may enjoy. Pay attention. Your calling—is calling.

You are not here
For the reasons you think you are.
Your relationships are not here
For the reasons you think they are.
You are learning—they are teaching.
You are teaching—they are learning.

Relationships are reciprocal interactions. Each brings what the other needs. The lesson is the same—detachment. Attachment brings suffering by seeking to manipulate the free will of others. This surfaces when others choose to be who they are, despite who you want them to be.

Detachment allows one to experience the reality of relationships exactly as they are. Learning this serenity is the purpose of their role in your life.

Growth is determined by the mental anguish you are willing to release. When you are ready to understand the cause of distress, you are also ready to move past it.

Just because you hurt doesn't mean you're ready to stop. Anguish is the natural by-product when personal opinion overshadows wisdom as the cementing factor in relationships. Attachment to opinion is the origin of emotional discomfort. Healing happens when you summon the courage to relinquish what's hurting you.

There is only one time—now.

There is only one life—consciousness.

There is only one error—misunderstanding.

There is only one limit—fear.

There is only one sin—separation.

There is only one bondage—attachment.

And finally, one purpose—evolution.

Separating from your source over time creates bondage to error, limiting life by misunderstanding its purpose.

Relationships

are easily reduced to a feeling.
You think the relationship caused the feeling?
No, it is the feeling that caused the relationship.

Feelings are the result of what you are believing.
Relationships merely confirm the feelings.

Anger is a reaction to obstacles
Blocking your path to freedom.
Though you blame others,
The obstacle resides in every attachment
You are unable to release.

Anger results from an inability to detach from
a limiting perspective. Practicing detachment
allows Life to flow freely and impersonally,
leaving peace of mind in its wake.

To enter freedom, enter the flow.

Severing ties with the oneness of Life creates a separate identity called "the i." You know: "i want— i think— i have— i know—" and countless other claims the i makes for itself. Separated from its source, the intent of the i is to block peace of mind.

Establishing itself apart from the Universe, the scope of the i is severely limited. Still, it masquerades with full authority over the life of the one who accepts it. You can always recognize the presence of the i because it maintains the inflexible viewpoint that something is "out of place." This attitude interprets everything as a problem that needs fixing. Shrouded in personal opinion mistaken for wisdom, it moves covertly or overtly toward a quick fix—that never happens.

Far from offering a solution, stress is all the i confers to the mind because it can never fix what is not broken.

If the i understood that all manifestation is caused (not coincidental), separation from its source would be healed. To this end, every day is laden with healing opportunities, should you choose to enter this practice.

Until then, the i designs new stress to experience.

A birth-day is a gift you grant yourself when you grow beyond a former limitation. Experiencing this growth celebrates life's purpose.

Far from an annual event, birth-days continually unfold when learning experiences are actually learned.

There is no shortage of anything in the Universe except the understanding that brings it to pass.

This Kingdom of Heaven lies just on the other side of limiting beliefs. It is the **i** that blocks this understanding.

A personality's dominant trait is characterized by its habitual response to Life. Opposition or acceptance creates energy that is either serene and confident, or confused and fearful.

One's state of mind is characterized by one's trust in the Universe.

I forgot is too often a mental excuse allowing the mind to negate what is not considered beneficial.

This forgetfulness allows the mind to indulge activities deemed more meaningful while ignoring the greater underlying truth:

The mind does not forget what it considers important.

If you truly have a desire, give it to yourself by accepting responsibility for its creation.

"Wanting" implies that you do not mentally possess the image of your desire, signaling the Universe to honor the belief that you do not have it.

Nurture expectant thoughts for intentions you design. Marshaling discipline to this commitment allows you to wait expectantly. Be not discouraged if, at first, you waver. Constantly practicing discipline proves your faith. Faith happens.

Seek ye first the Kingdom and your details will be worked out for you. Seek ye first the details and even more details appear.
When in doubt remember:
If you leave it alone, harmony takes care of it. If you take care of it, harmony leaves it alone.

At the unconscious level, the mind constantly edits its destiny. It is here that focused ideas are accepted as beliefs and empowered to manifest. Never static, this activity endures moment-to-moment. Whether to the benefit or detriment of the user, all utilize the power of acceptance to strengthen, abolish or create beliefs. Harnessing this genie is a rare realization.

What is repeatedly entertained as a reality will surely manifest as one. As a result, you find yourself physically performing what you mentally practice.

Mastering mental dominion is the answer to cherished dreams.

What you teach, you must first become, and you become only what you practice.

In reality, your practice is your teaching.

What you preach is neither here nor there.

Parenting is less a matter of raising children than it is raising consciousness. Your own.

Parenting is basically the practice of being who you truly are—in front of souls needing the experience of who you are. Beyond that, the Universe raises every child according to the Law of their being.

In the final analysis, you can only raise your awareness or consciousness. This growth carries the potential to ignite the growth of others. If understood as reciprocal teachers, children assist greatly in the raising of your consciousness.

Or not—depending on your parenting choices.

The Universe brings to you what comes to you. Whatever that is, it is a part of evolution being worked out. Your response to the moment is your contribution to the balancing that is taking place. This is also known as your lesson.

Each one is perfectly matched with the challenge most needed for their evolution. What confronts you is the opportunity to overcome a liability. Accept what you think you cannot. It is not so much the appearance you accept but the law that governs its manifestation.

You are a spiritual being with thoughts that wear physical forms.

Though parents name your body, your thoughts brand your identity. Each body wears a cloak of energy that defines its presence. This signature energy is the name you choose for yourself; it is who you really are. And this is what discerning souls recognize.

An error rightly understood is a blessing multiplied.

Misunderstood—it remains an error and multiplies anew.

Over and over, a familiar question repeats itself:
How can I change what is happening to me—now?

Strangely enough, acceptance is the first step. Choosing to accept the invitation to grow initiates the process of change. But commitment determines when the change takes place, gradually unfolding as you substitute personal responses for Universal responses. The more you practice this harmony, the more harmony you attract.

Change is just a choice away.

You always get the answer you want.

Of all available options, you will invariably choose the answer that matches the belief you already hold.
In truth, an answer is rarely sought,
Only confirmation of an existing belief.

You will always get the answer you want until you grow into the answer you need.

The surest way to birth a change
is to practice the change as if it were true.
Practice implies acceptance, saying to the Universe, "Here is where I stake my faith."

The Universe listens and delivers.

The reality you hold
Is the reality that unfolds.

The only thing happening to you is your belief
about what should happen to you.

You say you cannot find happiness?
Rejoice, for you have stumbled upon a guiding
truth.
Happiness wears a million faces and
Changes the moment you think you've found it.
A master of illusion, it cannot be found.

Feeling incomplete, the soul seeks relentlessly to
fill this void and cannot understand why outer
efforts avail little. Like the prodigal son, it fails
to see its emptiness as a constant reminder that
what it seeks is reconnection to the Source of its
being.

Returning to one's primal position fills the void,
and the joy that was sought finds you.

You understand only what you prepare yourself to understand, and this by the practice of listening. You listen to either the wisdom of heaven or the wisdom of earth—the wisdom of man or the wisdom of the Universe. Whichever you practice embeds in your consciousness as a certainty.

You understand that which supports your certainty.

Forgiveness is a gift that you give to yourself.
You choose a higher understanding in place of a lower one,
And behold—

You forgive the error in your thinking.

The question often surfaces, "Why do people act the way they do?" Careful examination shows that human activity consists almost exclusively of satisfying what it perceives as its deepest needs. Though relationships wear myriad disguises, the promise of security is usually the sustaining factor.

It is human to act human. But consciousness possesses a Universal self as well as a human self. The Universal self conducts affairs differently and cautions against the practice of chasing security. Instead, it encourages each to find security in the center of their being. Forsaking this instruction triggers an endless quest for security in a world that offers none, thus causing people to act the way they do.

It is all in the view they embrace of themselves.

Adults leave but two legacies: The best of themselves and the worst of themselves.

Children learn what they came here to learn, even when they become adults.

Tension is a symptom of over-attachment to the unimportant. The cousin to stress, it destroys your countenance in limitless ways. The good news is that you can always relinquish attachment to what injures you and substitute acceptance of that which does not.

Personal opinions lie at the root of all tension. Detachment spontaneously severs this distress.

What is right? And what is wrong?

Whatever you choose is right for you, and what is not chosen becomes wrong—for you. Your unique growth pattern makes your choices and assures that you grow in exactly the way that you choose.

The Law of Balance allows all selections, making each right by matching the energy of results to the energy of choices.

There is no right or wrong way. There's just the way you learn.

Watch what causes excessive emotions. The Universe is showing you a blind spot. Three things surface automatically: You will see without clarity, become vulnerable to another's advantage and burdened with guilt at the thought of acting independently.

Be leery of what prompts and promotes emotionalism or sentimentality. Currying favor with neither, the Universe offers the middle road as the shining template—otherwise known as impersonal balance, which is Love.

Would you behold
the face of your soul?
Examine your beliefs.
Would you behold your beliefs?
Examine your judgments about the people, places and things in your world.

Each soul is an intricate pattern of judgments, which is no more than the accumulated energy of all you have accepted. Studying these findings introduces you to your soul.

Hearing guidance
that is not experienced
is the same as not hearing guidance.
Both fail to pierce the unknown for revelations
are not answers until practiced.

What is unknown lies on the other side of
consensus reality. To enter, one must be bereft
of all preconceived ideas and mental safety
nets. Alone, the mind proceeds with certainty,
following only the light that shares itself. The
experience illumines what was hidden, and the
unknown becomes known.

When you remove accumulated
misunderstandings from the center of your life,
all that remains is peace.

This at-one-ment with the Universe rebuilds
your life perfectly, naturally and spontaneously.

Your birth parents named your body to distinguish it from other bodies, but you choose your real name by the way you choose to grow. That name follows you as your energy.

The Universe recognizes the name you give yourself and separates you from energy unlike your own. In this way it returns to you only what you have named for yourself.

Often the thought looms, "There is no evidence of progress." But evidence accompanies every step of your journey, for it is found in your ability to withhold judgments about the moment.

Progress is knowing what progress is.

Getting one's needs met is the basis of human interactions. Irrespective of the jurisdiction, this pervasive element colors relationships from birth to transition.

Realizing the unique needs of each person explains why the Universe behaves the way it does. Either way, human or universal, meeting needs remains the crux of Life.

What is success but having peace of mind?

Largely forgotten, peace of mind was actually the reason behind each struggle to succeed.

As such, success and failure are merely proximities to peace of mind.

You do not pray with
carefully selected words
But with your abiding attitude toward the source
of your being.

And prayers are always answered, for they are
fixed habits of response that will not fail to
attract the energy they possess.

Your most poignant lessons are found
in your closest relationships.

Emotionally charged, they persuade you to
mistrust the wisdom of inner guidance in favor
of continued habits of cultural conditioning. Pay
attention to what your loved ones are teaching.

Your response is the lesson.

What you seek seeks you
And will unerringly find you, in time.

Habitual thinking creates a direct path to your door. Arriving, it will enter without knocking. Be prepared to entertain the guest you invited.

There is a place for everything, and everything is in it.

To remain all-that-is, the Universe must contain not only the reality of all things but also the possibility of all things. The stupendous task of keeping it all balanced is achieved effortlessly through the Law of cause and effect.

The Universe communicates with each in the language they best understand.

Essentially, there are two languages, harmony and dissonance. Your experiences return in the language you are speaking.

Everyone teaches one subject with absolute authority—
the lesson of who they are.
Their world is a classroom of students responding to the teaching.

Ultimately it is the teacher being taught.

If you must change who you are
to be accepted,
closely examine this acceptance.

You will see that it is only your willingness to be
manipulated that is being accepted.

You are a unique contribution to the
wholeness of Life, just the way you are. The
Universe totally accepts your contribution and
uses it lovingly and purposefully. Accepting your
self as you are is the lesson all parties must learn.

It is impossible to waste time. Now is the only time there is and belongs exclusively to the Universe. Every moment is used to achieve its purpose of evolution, and this through balance.

So relax. You are right where you are supposed to be, doing what you are supposed to be doing and receiving what is yours to receive. And whatever that is, you can be sure it is an opportunity to exchange personal thinking for Universal thinking. Nature does not know how to waste time.

Too much attention is paid to what cannot be changed and too little attention to what can.

Your mind is the only thing you can change. The Universe changes everything else to match it.

When ideas finally reach the level of belief, an amazing thing happens—the belief.

Neither plenty, poverty nor pathos can avert the lessons you have assigned to yourself. Each condition is a major part of your learning.

Each lesson reveals an issue where personal opinion replaces the wisdom of what is. This transgression causes feelings of dis-ease, alerting you that you are in the midst of a lesson you yourself designed. Surrendering attachment to personal views is the teaching behind all the lessons.

The relationship of the soul to its creator is the binding union of every life. It is the marriage that no man can put asunder.

So powerful is this marriage that physical unions mimic it with exact precision. Throughout life, you repeatedly partner with energy that matches your own. It may be people, places or things.

Ever wonder why advice never works? It cannot. You must do the work.

Advice introduces you to the process of transformation but cannot make you choose it. Commitment to the process is the work required of you. Your persistence alerts the Universe to begin a change that corresponds to your desire. Remember, the Universe wants for you what you want for yourself.

You must choose to know
the answers you seek.

Seeking is but a fraction of the journey.
Experiencing answers is the rest of it.

An argument never happens until
someone has to be right.

Next time you argue, ask yourself, "Why do I
have to be right?"

Why argue? You are both right, for each holds
the reality that is right for them. Further, it
is impossible to convince another of what is
foreign to their experience. And convincing
is the cause of the debate. Accepting this
understanding ends the argument.

"Thy will be done on earth as it is in heaven"
is the reigning Law of Life.

It is wise to become intimately acquainted with your will. The Law is.

We are always teaching ourselves
what we need to know
To grow.

The lessons do not choose us.

It is said that beauty is in the eye of the beholder, but the truth is, so is everything else.

The mind sees outwardly what it is inwardly.

Too often a positive goal is sabotaged by ineffective and sporadic faith.
Fear, on the other hand,
is uncontested faith,

which, therefore, programs it to happen.

Feelings paint the events that happen day-to-day.
You only feel what you believe to be true, and what you believe will most definitely happen.

It is useless to argue against the events of the day. They all arrive on time.

An understanding of the outer world is always faulty until reconciled with an understanding of the inner world.

The inner life parents the outer world, otherwise known as "the father and the son."

You are born to the family that most
shares your strengths and weaknesses. The ideal
goal of the unit is to strengthen the strengths
and weaken the weaknesses.

Your birth family is only the first of many. It is
here you first learn to wrestle the challenges
of strengths and weaknesses. In time you
will be moved to other relationships, but
make no mistake. The goal remains the same,
strengthening the strengths while weakening
the weaknesses. Growth is strength.

No experience in your life
is caused by another person.
Universal Law uses others to obey the
energy of your mind.

Relationships enter your life for the reason that
you summoned them. The reason is always
growth. What is there to learn? Unconditional
acceptance of the Law that governs
manifestation.

Attachment to illusion is the only bondage, occurring whenever one cannot release that which limits his growth.

Evolution is the resolution.

In essence, no one does anything wrong, for none can operate outside the Law. "Wrong" is the term used when cause and effect result in dissatisfaction instead of satisfaction.

Dissatisfaction is a profound message. It is Life's invitation to change.

There is no "problem" that will not respond to correction.

Trusting the world for answers is the correction needed. Seek ye first the kingdom of oneness, and what was a problem unravels. What's left is a peaceful mind.

Should you feel the urge to judge the moment, first ask yourself, "Why should it be other than what it is?"

The answer returns, "Only because you do not agree with it." That which is unacceptable to you is generally judged as "wrong." But is it? The growth process designs the moment, causing to happen exactly what needs to happen to extend healing to everyone concerned.

You will never understand in another what you do not first understand in yourself.

Essentially, all are the same, distinguished only by levels of awareness.

A soul's readiness to accept and integrate higher awareness determines its behavior patterns. Since all conform to this timeless principle, self-insight forms the basis for understanding one's neighbor.

What is truth?

What you feel is truth, for it is an existing reality. But truth happens as reality on both personal and Universal levels.

But of the two, only Universal reality is true everywhere all the time.

When in human form,
the Universe resides in you.
When form transitions,
you reside in the Universe.

There is never a separation,
unless you think there is.

When you come to the edge of all
you have learned and fail to receive what you
sought, it becomes obvious that what is needed
is something you have yet to learn.

The world teaches everything but how to trust
the Universe. This must be learned on your own,
one moment at a time. The freedom you seek is
there.

Depression is a
mind-set resisting evolution.
Frozen in a rigid thought pattern, it is a boulder
keeping the Spirit buried so that it cannot
create.

Reverse thinking cracks the ice. Frequent
practice thaws it. The entire process consists
of eliminating personal opinion about what is
happening in the moment. This elimination frees
the Spirit.

The energy of your mind is your only
real possession and, as such, is all that you will
ultimately take with you. Earth is the classroom
for learning about this energy and, once
evolved, this energy illumines the way home.

Home is a reality that sees the Divine in all
things. Some call it praying without ceasing.
In this discerning state of mind, you come to
know that death does not take you home—
understanding does.

Within every mind, the "i" stunts the birth of expansion and illumination.

A downward spiral, this "fall" is reversed only when the mind surrenders addiction to the personal life for an understanding of the impersonal life.

A committed desire for oneness with the Universe signals the birth of awakening.

The path of awakening is unique from one individual to the next because it requires dismantling only the obstacles they themselves created.

And then, only if you choose to. Your time line is your own. Eternity is patient.

The "problem" is never what's happening around you. Thinking there's a problem is the problem. Personal judgment is forever at the root of what troubles you.

Divine trust knows that what happens needs to happen for the healing of all involved. Though largely misunderstood, trust is a blessing of profound magnitude, contributing greatly to the healing taking place before you and—more importantly—within you. Notice how peaceful you are when you trust the wisdom of things as they are.

Every single time.

Experimenting

with cause and effect is the daunting task
of every soul, but even more compelling is
remembering why.

The accumulation of lifetime choices is stored
as the soul's DNA. This history is both ancient
and current. Here is the entire record of your
journey—the journey of separating from your
source. Reconnecting to the flow of the Universe
restructures your DNA. Restructuring DNA
evolves existence, an opportunity presented by
the earthly experience.

Some gaze upon life as a glass

half-empty, others, as a glass half-full. But
either conclusion is a personal judgment of
what is happening around you. This single
practice forgets the truth that both the glass and
its contents belong exclusively to the Universe.
And that means one thing—

The glass is balanced. Is it not?

Your entire life is determined by your relationship to the Universe.

Life teaches endless variations of a single theme. "Thy will be done on earth as it is in heaven." Infinite scenarios are designed to temper and master your response. The lesson is learned when acceptance without judgment is your dominant response.

It matters not how much you know,

It matters what you practice.

Begin training your wings. Practice flight.

Awakening to the Journey

As of this day, know that the Universe unfolds
itself perfectly.

Surrender the belief that you know what is best;
You only know what you desire.

What is best happens moment-to-moment
With a balance beyond mortal comprehension
Except that Life moves to the rhythm of cause
and effect.

Therefore, study the effect
That finds its way to your moment,
Knowing its cause is anchored in you,
Hidden no longer—now in full view.

Ask for Wisdom to understand what you see
And Wisdom explains its mystery.

"The journey you travel is through the mind.
Embedded beliefs are your own design.
Regardless of notions you've been told,
Beliefs you hold always unfold.
Decipher the Law that can't deceive—You only
receive what you first believe."

~D. Hall

About the Author

A medical professional with an interest in healing consciousness, the author advocates heightened awareness as a therapeutic tool for transformation and healing.

A lover of outdoors, jnana received during nature walks and meditation inspire writings aimed solely at supporting the awakening experience. With an easy down-to-earth approach, the author specializes in making the invisible visible.

Missives from the Universe introduces the basics of this timeless process.

www.ingramcontent.com/pod-product-compliance
Lightning Source LLC
LaVergne TN
LVHW011335080426
835513LV00006B/363